Be ReVITALized

Be ReVITALized
Michelle's Musings on Motherhood

By Michelle Kauenhofen

PRESCOTT PUBLISHING

Be ReVITALized: Michelle's Musings on Motherhood

Published by Prescott Publishing
3726 Woods Boulevard
Tyler, TX 75707
http://prescottpublishing.org

Cover image: Bahman Farzad
Cover design: Jennifer Flanders

ISBN: 978-1-938945-10-6
LCCN: 2014954289

Dedication

I dedicate this book to all the overwhelmed and struggling mommas out there who think they are failing or have lost hope. You are doing great, just keep going.

Contents

Acknowledgements

I acknowledge that the precious privilege of motherhood has taught me many things, including the depth of my capacity to love, the intensity and rawness of emotion, the all consuming definition of care and compassion, and the magnitude of my own personal sins and shortcomings.

Motherhood moves me to desire to be a better version of myself.

I am thankful for the gift that motherhood is, and beyond grateful for the beautiful souls I have tried to nurture and raise.

Motherhood has driven me to my knees many times over—and that is a great place to be.

Be ReVITALized
MOTHERHOOD THOUGHT FOR THE DAY: 1

You Are My Sunshine

*"The wind may howl and the dishes may pile,
But my whole world brightens when my baby smiles."*

I love how a baby's smile stops life in its tracks and brings total joy to the room.

What a privilege to sit and engage with a baby.

Truly, I think babies make the world go round.

Love,

Michelle

Love It!

I saw an Italian quote that read: *"Una buona Mamma vale cento maestre."*

Translated, this means: "A good mother is worth a hundred teachers."

Isn't that so true? In actuality, a mother is a one-of-a-kind, irreplaceable cornerstone in her child's life, forever.

When you feel overwhelmed, remember just how significant you are to your child's life. Did you know that a child is only a child for a very short time? The years pass quickly, so take the time to savour them.

Love,

Michelle

Letter to Mothers

Dear Precious Wives and Mothers,

I know sometimes it is hard. Sometimes we are criticized and judged. Sometimes we even question ourselves, and doubt our own abilities.

But here's the thing: It is not the critic that counts. It is easy to sit back and be a critic. But the critic will not know victory. It is by far better to actually be in the "ring," pouring forth effort, facing the struggles, striving (and sometimes erring), while spending all that we are for the worthiest cause.

We will know victory. Jesus set the example for us. Despite His critics, He poured Himself out for the greatest of causes. He is our inspiration. So likewise, we pour ourselves out for our families. In so doing, we are also triumphing in greatness. Nothing is more powerful, and nothing is more valuable here in our daily lives.

Approach today with renewed vigour, and silence any critical voices with your calm resolve. Don't make it your goal to please the critics, but to please the Lord and to glorify Him with your home, your family life, and your efforts.

Love,

Michelle

Be ReVITALized
MOTHERHOOD THOUGHT FOR THE DAY: 4

Imagine That!

You know that feeling of heart-bursting, joyful tears and welling-up pride you feel for your child? Sometimes over the smallest of achievements or the slightest of progress?

The LORD feels the same way for us, but even more completely!

God loves us beyond measure. It fills us up to running over. Out of the abundance of that love, may we learn to love others deeply and unconditionally.

Love,

Michelle

Be ReVITALized
MOTHERHOOD THOUGHT FOR THE DAY: 5

What Do You Think?

Do you ever feel like what you do at home is insignificant in the big scheme of things? Perhaps you think you could better serve the Lord by doing something else, something different, something that seems more important. Maybe you secretly long for something with more recognition or possibly even some pay?

Don't be deceived; your pay is incalculable. Your impact on future generations cannot even be tallied! The payoff is everlasting and eternal, unlike a physical paycheque that is quickly used up and gone. Serving your family is one of the most significant things you can do with your life. Not only are the payoffs eternal and the impact powerful, but all your efforts are noticed and appreciated by the KING OF KINGS!

How's that for recognition? Your submission to His will is invaluable. He loves the example you set as a loving wife and mother. He loves how you teach the women around you to tend the home. He loves how you teach your children His ways. He loves how you meet your husband's needs. Your reward will be massive, dear mother, both in this life and the next. So if you are "only" a stay at home mom, be proud and grateful. Not all are as blessed as you.

Love,

Michelle

Mary and Martha

There is a common battle that we mothers face. I like to call it the Martha/Mary battle. We can so easily become consumed by the never-ending demands of running our homes and families. We naturally focus on all the very necessary things that have to be done, but such a focus can lead to our not having enough time left after everything else to enjoy our husbands and children.

I've noticed this battle within myself, especially during our recent move. We must regularly pace ourselves, and balance our Martha tendencies with our Mary point of view. After all, the work does not all have to get done this minute. Take time to just *be* each day. Those are moments that are never regretted.

Love,

Michelle

Be ReVITALized
MOTHERHOOD THOUGHT FOR THE DAY: 7

Touch a Life!

As our children grow, we tend to hug and embrace them less frequently. In our culture, too, it is almost too personal to reach out and embrace people.

Today I encourage you to touch a life—literally. I had a 60+ aged woman tell me one day how nice it was to just have someone touch her, even on the arm. She missed being touched, now that she lived alone.

Touch people, speak life into them, and impact them. Lift them up with your embrace and your words. Make it a habit. It's a good one. Go out of your comfort zone. Who wants to live in the comfort zone anyway? It's a dangerous place to stay.

Love,

Michelle

True Beauty

Seriously, is there anything more beautiful than a pregnant woman? My heart is filled with joy and appreciation when I see a bulging belly walk by. It is a sign that the Lord continues to replenish the earth, and it is so beautiful. Don't you think so too?

Bless and encourage pregnant mommas that you meet. Put a smile on their face. It is a mighty work to grow a new life.

Love,

Michelle

Be ReVITALized
MOTHERHOOD THOUGHT FOR THE DAY: 9

Worth Repeating

I love JC Ryle and thought this was worth sharing. He writes:

> *"I know that you cannot convert your child. I know well that they who are born again are born, not of the will of man, but of God. But I know also that God says expressly, 'Train up a child in the way he should go,' and that He never laid a command on man which He would not give man grace to perform. And I know, too, that our duty is not to stand still and dispute, but to go forward and obey. ... It is just in the going forward that God will meet us. The path of obedience is the way in which He gives the blessing. We have only to do as the servants were commanded at the marriage feast in Cana, to fill the water-pots with water, and we may safely leave it to the Lord to turn that water into wine."*
>
> *– JC Ryle*

I especially love that last line.

Love,

Michelle

Be ReVITALized
MOTHERHOOD THOUGHT FOR THE DAY: 10

Losing Sleep

Another restless, sleepless night spent nursing fulltime with a baby attached? *Awesome!*

How many nights in my life will I have like that? Too few, I am sure.

I have deliberately lost sleep over much less significant things, so I choose to be grateful as I recognize how short and precious the season is that I am in.

Love,

Michelle

Be ReVITALized
MOTHERHOOD THOUGHT FOR THE DAY: 11

Prayer for the Mother

Dear Heavenly Father,

I thank You for Your grace and mercy upon me. I thank You that You often use the least of these, and that my feelings of doubt or inadequacy do not ever thwart Your plans.

I pray that You would fill me with Your Spirit and enable me by Your grace. I want to be a sweet wife and mother who is cherished and remembered fondly by her family, rather than the harsh, complaining, stressed-out woman I can sometimes be.

Forgive me when I lose sight of Your truth and focus instead on worldly cares. Help me to see and know Your Truth. Strengthen me and my faith, O Lord, and help me and my household to walk in righteousness.

In Jesus name, Amen.

Love,
Michelle

Gourmet Dinner

Do the children ever turn up their noses to your new meals?

A wise friend once told me that the difference between an "unappealing" meal, and a "gourmet" one is serving it twice.

I have found that to be true. As long as I keep at it, my family eventually begins to enjoy it.

Persistence pays off—in meals and in much, much more, like prayer.

Love,

Michelle

Parents Need Assistance in Their Mighty Task!

We need a community, don't we? The people and friends with whom our families and our children are surrounded make a huge impact on all of our lives.

Pray daily for your children to be surrounded by great and godly peers. May they point their friends toward the Lord, and may their friends do the same for them.

We need a community, but not just any community. We need a godly community.

Pray for it.

Love,
Michelle

Ears Perk Up

Children never outgrow the desire to hear words of praise and affirmation from their parents. I was reminded of this fact the other night when Cam and I took our oldest four children out for dinner recently. They are now 21, 19, 18, and 15, but they groaned and looked somewhat mortified when I said I was going to speak a blessing to each one of them right there at the restaurant table. I proceeded to tell them, one at a time, specific ways that they'd been blessing me. I told them things I'm proud of in their lives and things that impressed me about them. I spoke of things that I loved and adored about each one of them, too.

Although they all originally thought it was a horrible idea, and I know that I put them on the spot and way out of their comfort zones, I also know it was worth it. I sure had their full and complete attention, and their unbroken eye contact when I spoke. All their ears just perked right up! What a great reminder for me, as truthfully, more of what proceeds from my mouth to my children is correction, teaching, and training, rather than praise and adoration. Want your child's attention? Speak blessings and affirmations, and they will be sure to listen. Perk up the ears in your house today, even if it takes someone out of their comfort zone!

Love,

Michelle

Be ReVITALized
MOTHERHOOD THOUGHT FOR THE DAY: 15

Bringing Joy

Even in crowded and busy stores, smiling children bring joy to tense shoppers.

Today amongst the mobs in the grocery store, where people were looking grim, Solana (our four-year-old) announced to me, "Momma, everybody likes me!"

They all had a smile for the happy little girl, even though they didn't appear to be otherwise enjoying the crowds or their errands.

Children spread joy and smiles everywhere they go. Thank God for little ones!

Love,

Michelle

Embrace the New Normal

Motherhood has many seasons, each with new challenges. No sooner do we adjust to one season than a new one emerges.

The baby grows, a new baby comes, a toddler becomes a child ready for school, a tween becomes a teen, a high school student graduates, a college student studies, a young adult needs direction, a wedding to plan, a grandbaby or two join the family.

Life is so fluid, and often we forget how transient each season really is. "Normal" family life is forever re-adjusting, and we do well to continually embrace each "new normal" that presents itself.

Sometimes there is a season that allows for a more orderly home, sometimes there is a season that does not. Both are seasons, both are normal, and both are good. Embrace whatever season you are in whole-heartedly and pack every great memory you can into it. Before you know it, that season will be behind you and a new one will have begun.

Love,

Michelle

16

Be ReVITALized
MOTHERHOOD THOUGHT FOR THE DAY: 17

Babies Aren't the Only Ones Growing Up

Tonight as I went to give my two-year-old a bath, I grabbed the community paper to read. Once I got in the bathroom and started her bath though, I immediately began washing the sink, the toilet, the floor, the counters, and then I noticed the paper.

I smiled. Why read a paper when I can make the bathroom a more pleasant place for everyone to visit, I thought to myself. Then I remembered how a younger me would have reacted. I would have complained how awful it was to not have time to read it, as there was always too much work for me to do. I would have resented that people in the house weren't cleaning up after themselves the way I would like, and the grumbling in my head and heart would have continued into a pity party and likely ruined that bath time.

How silly of me! It is great to grow and learn, isn't it?

Love,

Michelle

Be ReVITALized
MOTHERHOOD THOUGHT FOR THE DAY: 18

Hold Them Close

Babies just want to be with their mommas, but before you know it, they are too big to lift off the ground!

The snuggle-close years of sleeping near momma are precious and short. Enjoy them while you can!

Love,

Michelle

Be ReVITALized
MOTHERHOOD THOUGHT FOR THE DAY: 19

The Power of Praying

Parents need to lean on the Lord for the mighty and awesome task of training the next generation:

> *"Thank you for my children, Lord. I know they are a gift from you. Daily I need your strength and wisdom to train them in the way they should go. Give me patience and a joyful heart. Let me be an example of your love and forgiveness. Thank you for the honour of being a parent. Amen."*

Love,

Michelle

Be ReVITALized
MOTHERHOOD THOUGHT FOR THE DAY: 20

Shouting from the Rooftops

One of my favourite scriptures is 1 Samuel 2:21, *"And the LORD visited Hannah, so that she conceived."*

The LORD has visited me, and I have conceived many times in my life, although not every conception has resulted in a live birth.

After having experienced several pregnancy losses, we are absolutely over-the-moon, shouting-from-the-rooftops elated and completely rejoicing and, of course, coveting all prayers on our behalf for a healthy baby and an uncomplicated, full-term pregnancy each and every time we are visited.

We always feel so blessed to be visited, continually amazed at the excitement the news of each positive pregnancy test brings. Each day we carry a new life is a day of marvel, gratitude and joy, worthy of celebration.

Love,

Michelle

Be ReVITALized
MOTHERHOOD THOUGHT FOR THE DAY: 21

Are You Facing Curveballs?

We mommas want all to be perfect and delightful for our children. It is our natural nurturing instinct to protect them. When our children are happy and healthy, we are at peace. But when life throws a curveball, it can break our hearts. We cannot stand it when our babies (of any age) suffer, because we just love them so much.

We must be strong in such times though, and we must remain thankful. After all, we are grateful to be mommas, and we can be grateful for our lot, whatever it may be. It is a privilege to walk through life alongside our children, through all the ups and downs. Even with hurting hearts, we can always choose to be positive. In this way, they too will see the strength, the peace, and the stability of God's grace. So, although it may not always be easy, let's embrace the trials we face. Let's tackle our problems with a trusting and positive spirit, and God will be glorified

Love,

Michelle

The Psalm 128 Life

Families with several children are often bombarded with comments and questions, and wonder how to best respond. Listen carefully to the words of Psalm 128:

> *"Blessed is every one that feareth the LORD; that walketh in his ways. For thou shalt eat the labour of thine hands: happy shalt thou be, and it shall be well with thee. Thy wife shall be as a fruitful vine by the sides of thine house: thy children like olive plants round about thy table. Behold, that thus shall the man be blessed that feareth the LORD."*

Those who fear the Lord and walk in His ways shall: 1) benefit from their labour, 2) be happy and well, 3) have fruitful wives (have you ever noticed how a vine grows and spreads along the wall of a house?), 4) have children around their tables. I didn't make this up. The Psalm says so. Next time someone makes a comment to me about my 12 children, or my wanting more children, I shall answer like this: "We are just trying to live the Psalm 128 life."

That should get them reading the Scriptures, and what will there be to debate after that?

Love,

Michelle

Masterpiece

Momma, you are a one-of-a-kind, beautifully handcrafted, and rare original for whom there is no compare.

You are absolutely irreplaceable and precious.

Walk in that truth today.

Love,

Michelle

Be ReVITALized
MOTHERHOOD THOUGHT FOR THE DAY: 24

The Best Days of Your Life

Time. It shows no favoritism, and yet it molds each of us.

As a young mother, I longed to take a break from my responsibilities and just think about myself, as I did prior to motherhood.

As an older mother now, I find I can barely stand to miss a second away from my children. I have seen how fleeting the time is, how very quickly it passes, and I want to savor every moment with every single child at every stage.

I used to dream of having an entire day off, but now when I feel overwhelmed, I just need a tiny break—like a quick bath or a short workout.

Remember that you are always evolving as a mother. Be mindful of the fact that your feelings do change over time. Regardless of how hard parenting seems at this point in time, someday you will look back at the business of young motherhood and fondly recall that these truly were the best days of your life. Savor them.

Love,

Michelle

Who Is Spoiled?

My dear friend wrote this:

"Everyday I hold him till he falls asleep....

"No, I'm not spoiling him.

"The definition of spoil: Spoil (verb)

1. *to damage severely or harm.*
2. *to diminish quality of*
3. *to impair, damage, or harm the character by unwise treatment, excessive indulgence.*

"Definitely not spoiling."

I love it! I think she is the one excessively indulging as she gets all those amazing snuggles from her baby.

Who is spoiled? It really all depends on your definition.

Love,

Michelle

We Look Out for Each Other

One of the most beautiful things about families is how they work so lovingly together.

When travelling in Mexico, I saw an impoverished mother nursing her baby, while her young son played nearby. Her oldest daughter, who must have been about eight, tended so lovingly to both her brother and her mother, so that the mother could continue to sit and nurse the baby. The daughter was so amazing and so grown up as she did her very best to serve her family.

How powerful it is to watch the family work together! It makes me wonder how anyone can think that another sibling is not a blessing. That family moved my heart in their clear love for each other.

Bless them, Lord.

Love,

Michelle

Mother's Day Musings

As a younger momma, Mother's Day would often find me longing for a day to myself, away from my seemingly never-ending household and familial responsibilities. I also had grand expectations for gifts that would show me how valuable my sacrifice and service were.

Now, as a *somewhat* older momma, I absolutely love to just be with my children. All the little things they make for me mean so much more than they once did, because I now recognize these tokens for what they are: my children sharing their hearts and their adoration—for li'l ole undeserving me.

Wow. *Just wow.* So much to appreciate! And before you know it, they are too big for such gifts, and what I once almost disregarded ends.

Mother's Day reminds me of how amazing my life is, not because of gifts or recognition, but simply because I was given life and was blessed to give life, and together we all have the privilege of sharing life, love, and laughter.

Love,

Michelle

Children Give Big Boosts

Sometimes a mother feels tired, and sometimes even a little overwhelmed. What does a mother feel most often though?

The warming of her heart from the unabashed love her children offer her.

Nothing boosts a mother's day more than the joy her children brings her with the little things they say and do.

The other day, one of my daughters sent me a text when I was very far away. She knew I was with another mother at the time, and so she wrote, "Don't tell the friend you're with, but I think you are the prettiest mom ever. I love you."

They are always boosting us up, aren't they? What a joy!

Love,

Michelle

Be ReVITALized
MOTHERHOOD THOUGHT FOR THE DAY: 29

Milestones

In our house, some would say that something strange has happened. When our baby reaches a new milestone, you hear a round of "Oh, no's!"

You see, everyone is so thrilled to have a baby in the house again. Yet they are also very aware that perhaps this one will be our last. So whenever Kythan grows a little more towards toddlerhood and away from babyhood, they all exclaim, "Oh, no!"

"Oh, no! He has teeth!"

"Oh no, he's sitting up already!"

"Oh no, he's eating solid food so soon!"

"Oh no, he is sleeping almost through the night!"

These are indeed days that fly by all too fast. I'm so glad all our children realize that and appreciate every moment, if not every milestone.

Love,

Michelle

Be ReVITALized
MOTHERHOOD THOUGHT FOR THE DAY: 30

We Need Better Advertising

The other day, I was glancing through an in-flight magazine on an airplane and saw an ad for permanent birth control. The woman in the ad was pictured with a caption that read, "I love being done having kids."

What a pity! It really made me angry. Where are the ads that promote childbearing or child raising? Our populations are dwindling, and embracing children is a most fulfilling and amazing way to strengthen our nations and serve our Lord. If I had the finances, there would be full color ads in every magazine and newspaper, promoting the truly glorious life: a life of nurturing and embracing children, through every possible means—adoption, pregnancy, foster care, you name it. Can you see my ad? Smiling parents sitting around a table full of children or walking hand-in-hand to church, with the headline, "We love children, and we'd love more." Wouldn't that be beautiful? Then everyone would see it and be impacted. Seeing the ad would make them want a house full of children to share their lives with—and then our problem of dwindling populations would be solved! I guess for now, we'll just have to be live, walking ads, shining out the best way to live life. We are making an impact just by existing. Children are a blessing, in every way, all the time.

Love,

Michelle

Be ReVITALized
MOTHERHOOD THOUGHT FOR THE DAY: 31

Story Worth Sharing

My friend shared this with me and I love it:

"I saw an incredibly beautiful thing today, and I just had to share it. I took the kids to the pool, and we had a great time. While we were there, an incredibly overweight lady came in. She struggled getting into the pool, and I thought how brave she was to be there, among so many in-shape parents and children (not counting myself among them). Anyway, as she was getting into the pool, I realized that she had her son with her. Her older teen, very handicapped son with her. The tenderness and care she showed to him, with all the young children looking at him and asking their parents about him—well, it was just overwhelming. She talked softly and sweetly to him, stayed right there with him, quietly talked him through a problem with one of these little children. Always smiling, always gentle. Yes, strengths come in many different forms. Beauty at it's best. Thank you, Lord, for that beautiful momma and her sweet spirit. Much to appreciate if you have the eyes to see it."

Both that momma and her son are blessed. Praise God they have each other.
Love,

Michelle

Embracing the Attitude

Embracing children is an attitude. It means that whether you are able to birth, adopt, foster, mentor, or not, you embrace children as a most precious blessing.

Embracing children does not mean that we will all have large families, or that we will all be able to adopt, foster, or have opportunity to mentor.

It does mean that our attitude toward children is abundantly warm and welcoming. Our attitude will reflect God's heart toward children, not the world's. We will not view children as burdens, nuisances, drains or liabilities. We will view children as esteemed, valuable, precious, worthy of our time and resources.

Even if we ourselves are not able to parent, we still will enjoy the blessing of the children that touch our lives. We must counter the world's attitude toward children with God's attitude toward children, regardless of whether we ourselves are fertile or not. Children must be treated as the blessing they are, and our attitudes will speak volumes to the watching world around us.

Love,

Michelle

The Best Gift

Do you realize that the very best gift ever given was a baby?

The best gift God ever gave us was a newborn baby. This baby was better than life itself, since this baby offered eternal life to us.

Similarly, the best gift we can ever give or be given is a baby. No gift on earth matches the preciousness of a baby.

Of course, human babies will never offer us what the Christ baby offers, but that doesn't diminish the fact that the very best gifts come in the form of babies. I am always thrilled when I hear of a conception, because a new life, a new baby, an eternal soul, is the very best gift on earth.

Always celebrate babies and all the potential that they hold.

Love,

Michelle

Be ReVITALized
MOTHERHOOD THOUGHT FOR THE DAY: 34

Irreplaceable You

Sometimes the demands of home and family life make a mother feel pulled in too many directions. Yet this is not a bad thing, this is a great thing! This testifies to the high significance of her role.

The amazing truth of motherhood is that a mother can and does meet multitudes of needs each day. She is a worker like no other, rising to the challenges of each situation, regardless of the personal sacrifice involved. This is one of the beautiful ways she exemplifies Christ to the world.

Each of her days is filled with accomplishing so very much, and each new day brings more to do. She is not to be pitied for being in such high demand, but rather praised. She is absolutely irreplaceable!

Employees in the workforce strive to be irreplaceable in order to secure their jobs. They never want work to run out. An irreplaceable worker is envied, valued, praised, and never pitied. That is you, dear Mother. Your job is not only secure, but eternally important. You are irreplaceable and highly esteemed!

Love,

Michelle

Master Chef

I can go to the finest restaurant and order from their menu, but I am limited to whatever is on that menu.

In my home, I not only create the menu, I also prepare, select, season, and serve the dish however I like. I am the master chef in our home, with all of the creative freedom I like. It is such an exciting opportunity, and so filled with variety.

Each day anew grants us a fresh opportunity to create nourishing and tasty dishes for our families. It is an honour and a privilege, granting us all kinds of creative expression.

Enjoy your master chef role today, regardless of your ingredients. Have fun with it, and train your children to embrace the excitement that a kitchen offers.

Love,

Michelle

A Very Godly Message

My friend's mother is one of the most loving grandmothers that I have ever met. She recently returned from a trip to Hawaii, where she attended a church service with a beautiful female choir and traditional Hawaiian music. There was a baby crying in the service, and many in the congregation were turning their heads, beginning to wonder when that mother would take the baby out.

Then the minister said straight from the pulpit, "I love to hear babies in the church. Babies belong here. This is a baby born in the congregation, and she belongs here with us."

This sweet grandma cried as she retold the story to me, and said how ashamed she was of thinking that the precious mother and baby were disruptive. She was moved and impressed with the minister's correct opinion on the high value of children.

I think that congregation heard a very godly message that day, don't you?

Love,

Michelle

You're Having a Baby?

No, actually you are having a once-in-a-lifetime human soul who will live for all eternity.

You are carrying, or have delivered, a more than rare, utterly unique individual. This person possesses an unmatched combination of gifts and qualities that have never before been seen so blended together.

This unique awesomeness is packaged in a tiny person that has never existed before, and will never, ever be replicated.

It's a big deal and is well worth pouring your life into.

Love,

Michelle

Grow a Forest

Every now and then you hear a new one. Yesterday a young lady said to me, "You're not growing a family tree, you're growing a forest!"

I love that!

I told her that I hope to grow a massive forest and take over Canada. We all had a good laugh.

(Incidentally, my maiden name is Forrest.)

Love,

Michelle

Everybody Else?

"Why don't we go to school like everybody else?" asked my eight-year-old girl today.

"We are homeschoolers, that's why," I answered. "We don't want to be like 'everybody else."

The pull is very strong on every front to be just like 'everybody else.' It is definitely a challenge to be different.

I'm trying to foster a sense of excitement in our children to be unlike 'everybody else' in a myriad of ways.

Just another one of those amazing parenting opportunities that life holds.

Love,

Michelle

Be ReVITALized
MOTHERHOOD THOUGHT FOR THE DAY: 40

Lift Someone Up

Today at the gas pumps, I spontaneously started a conversation with the pregnant lady at the next pump. I told her that she was one of my most favorite shapes.

She told me that she was expecting twins and also had a 2-year-old and a 3-year-old at home. She said her husband says they are now done.

I advised her to not decide anything permanently, as they would very likely long for a baby in the house again sometime down the road, in the future. I reminded her how precious a time in life it is, when a baby is in the house.

She nodded in agreement.

I shared her how I wished I could be expecting twins, too. I bet she rarely heard that type of encouragement. She seemed pleased, and then complimented me, saying I looked good for having so many children. I told her I would be happiest to look like her and be having twins.

It was just a random blessing for blessing conversation. I love those divine little encounters.

Love,

Michelle

Family Time

It is so easy to be busy and focused on everything but the present moment.

I am constantly trying to keep in the forefront of my mind the fact that each moment is exceedingly precious and a potential long-term memory.

Savour your moments, Mommas. They'll never pass again.

Love,

Michelle

Be ReVITALized
MOTHERHOOD THOUGHT FOR THE DAY: 42

When Momma Slacks

When Momma slacks, things can change quick—and usually not for the better. I should know, as I had been extremely ill for almost a week, and could only manage life from my bed.

Although the family did manage quite well in my absence, there were many behaviors that needed addressing. In my sick and slack state, things had been left unattended. However, all slackness must come to an end, and appropriate actions must be taken once again. After all, Momma's job is just too important.

Just as slackness in the diet creeps pounds on the scale and unhealthiness to the body, so slackness in Momma creates a need for training and discipline. As soon as health returned, things needed to be addressed. A momma reigns as a queen, and as such, she must govern with authority. If you've been slacking, it is high time to lead, and run the home as you know it needs. We do create the atmosphere. It is a high and noble calling that requires the best of us. We indeed will reap a great harvest as we sow in godly instruction. Give it all you've got—and be blessed with results

Love,

Michelle

Change the World

Sure we can change the world by helping the poor and needy and serving the mission field. Sure we can change the world by giving of our time and resources.

But we can also change the world each and every day without ever leaving our homes.

We do this by showing our family the power of love and the truth of the Gospel. We raise up and influence generations that can trust the love of God and know the love of Mother.

We change the world every day by simply being an example of a loving wife and momma.

Love,

Michelle

Every Day You Tell a Story

A couple was watching our family for a while yesterday, and they started asking questions. The usual ones came up, like how many children do you have, what does your husband do, do you school at home, and how are you still sane, is it a religious thing, what about teenagers, etc.

By the end of the conversation, they told us that they were getting married this fall, and that they had been afraid of having any children at all. The lady said she found us completely inspiring, and they both remarked that they would rethink their whole concept of children.

Isn't that great? Praise the Lord, and let Him continue His mighty work in the hearts of people everywhere. Every day that we live we tell a story that others are watching.

Love,

Michelle

Be ReVITALized
MOTHERHOOD THOUGHT FOR THE DAY: 45

Center of the Universe

Isn't it amazing that no matter what else is going on around them, babies are completely fixated on their mothers?

To be a mother is to be the Center of the Universe to another precious person. What a privilege!

Love,

Michelle

Be ReVITALized
MOTHERHOOD THOUGHT FOR THE DAY: 46

Too Old for What?

Many people argue that they are too old for more children, and so they choose to not have any more. I hear things like, "I do not want a teenager in the house when I am in my sixties!" or "I will be old and retired before they are even married!" or "I am in my forties, I am too old for babies."

Funny thing is though, that these same people do not think they are too old for the workforce. They willingly work into their sixties or even their seventies. Clearly, they are not too old to work.

Most times they are not too old to raise children either. They have simply made a choice.

I am glad we have examples of some Biblical matriarchs that were old, and yet were still thrilled to raise children. Wish there were more like them living near me today. Wouldn't that be wonderful?

Love,

Michelle

Be ReVITALized
MOTHERHOOD THOUGHT FOR THE DAY: 47

Metamorphosis

The day I became a mother, the world not only welcomed a brand new person into it, but also a newly transformed person.

Motherhood transformed me into someone immensely more loving, more selfless, and more giving than I had ever been before.

And that was just the beginning. I actually wondered if I really knew what love was before I became a mother, as the love I felt was so powerful, I had nothing else to compare it to.

How can anyone diminish the power of motherhood? It is magnificently huge, transforming, and all encompassing. There is nothing else like it.

Love,

Michelle

47

The Best Opportunity

Motherhood is a calling, a privilege, and a gift. It is our legacy. It is what we embrace and pour ourselves into.

It is not burdensome. It is not an onerous list of unending tasks to complete. It is not some half-hearted thing we do on the side of other things.

Motherhood is a most powerful and significant calling. We have the opportunity to be in a loving relationship with a precious one-of-a- kind creation from the very hand of God Himself. We are granted guardianship, friendship and mentorship with an eternal soul whom we have the joy of sharing all of life with. It is the most amazing thing!

What could be a better use of our time? How can it ever be thought of as less than what it truly is? To be in relationship with our children and grandchildren throughout our lives with the ability to love and minister to them is absolutely the best of all opportunities.

Love,

Michelle

Feeling Tired?

You know those days that are ridiculously busy with non-stop demands that leave you wiped out at the end of the night?

Of course you do.

Well, don't go to bed feeling defeated. Go to bed feeling victorious! You have survived another day and accomplished tons of tasks. You have probably done more than you even thought possible, even if most of your day was focused on assisting a needy little person.

You nailed it!

So it is quite natural for you to feel tired and ready to sleep—so you'll be able to start over tomorrow. Time to replenish.

The victorious life we live takes energy! You are strong, you are capable, you are tough, you are Mother.

Love,

Michelle

Re-Focus

Today while running errands at Home Depot, one of the gentleman who was assisting me started up a friendly conversation. When he realized that I had 12 children, he said, "Wow, I only have two and they drive me crazy!"

This is such a common comment, isn't it? I responded, "Yes, children do drive us crazy sometimes, but they also often make our lives worth living, don't they?"

He immediately responded with positivity, agreeing that what I said was very true. We had a lovely chat, and I think it helped that I agreed with him about the struggles of child rearing before I turned the perspective around.

Our goal is always to lovingly promote the proper view of children, regardless of how many children one has or does not have. I think part of the reason families are small nowadays is because that gentleman's view is prevalent, and supersedes the biblical truth of the blessing of children. We need to re-focus continually.

Love,

Michelle

Be ReVITALized
MOTHERHOOD THOUGHT FOR THE DAY: 51

Comment Cards

Mothers of many often hear less than encouraging comments. Over the years, I have stored a couple of good ones in my memory bank and deliberately discarded the rest.

My favorite funny one was: "Wow, I am a mere mortal. You must be super human!"

The sweetest one was, "Really? You are seriously my hero!"

Don't let the negativity of others drag you down. Keep your mind focused on the good comments that come around and on the good things God's word says about having children.

"Whatever is of good report... think on these things."

Love,

Michelle

Interruptions?

When I was a young Momma, I would feel annoyed when I was trying to accomplish some baking or cleaning, and a little one would interrupt me and demand my attention. Now that I am an older Momma, I am happy to stop my work when a little one wants to give me a hug, or show me something. I feel privileged that they want my attention. It will not always be like this.

Taking that moment to focus on my child gives us both such pleasure, and the work still gets done soon enough. I look back and wonder why I ever got so worked up about these interruptions in the first place! It is thrilling when some little person wants my attention, so why did I get so frustrated?

Isn't it funny how perspectives change? That is why it is so important to not make decisions based on feelings, since feelings are always changing.

Love,

Michelle

Be Generous

From one busy momma to another, I would like to encourage all of us to be very generous. Amongst all the demands, the stress, the schedule disruptions, and the busyness, let's give more. More than usual—more than you even think you can.

Give the gift of what I will call the "generosity of grace." It will make the days sweeter and far more memorable. Pour it out and lavish your loved ones with it.

Grace. It's free, but not easy.

I know you can do it, and you will go to bed so much more at peace with yourself when you do.

Love,

Michelle

Sacrificial Parenting

A disturbing line of reasoning seems to be permeating our culture when it comes to parenting difficult teens. The logic goes something like this: "You can't change a person who refuses to change. You can't help someone who won't help himself. So step aside and let their foolishness run its course."

I disagree. Instead of following the world's faulty advice, I go to the Word for counsel. There I see the ultimate Parent's example. God looked at His children—so terribly lost, so persistent in sin, continually and horrifically failing in every way imaginable—and He basically said there is no sacrifice too great: He died to save His children. Why are so many parents ready to throw in the towel? There are always things that can be done, always new methods to explore, always new ways to approach a problem. There is always more prayer, more involvement, more love, more patience, and more hard, even heart-wrenching, work that can be done. We must never despair, but keep on trying. After all, our children are the future. They'll be raising the next generation. Our sacrifices are worth it. Let's follow the Father's example and not grow weary in parenting, even when trying times come. We must hope beyond hope and never, never, never give up.

Love,

Michelle

Be ReVITALized
MOTHERHOOD THOUGHT FOR THE DAY: 55

Sibling Bliss

One of the best parts of having siblings is that the baby becomes the center of attention.

Kythan regularly enjoys the attention of one of his sisters in particular, who loves to make him a bed and give him toys.

Bringing a baby into the family brings more joy to the siblings every time. They all take their turns playing, holding and showering him with love.

So thankful to have a baby in the house. The season is far too ridiculously short.

Love,

Michelle

Wild Party

The other night I was tucking two of my daughters into bed, and I saw that their room was a huge mess. I said, "Look at this room! Wow! You guys need to clean it up!"

My eight-year-old answered, "Mum, we had a wild party when those other children were over, and it got messy!"

I just had to laugh. How often I see mess, and they just see memories of grand fun. Once again, it was time to lighten up, and let life happen. Mess frequently happens when we are having fun, and there is always time to tidy up later. No need to get worked up about it.

It should actually bring a sense of joy to look around and know that so many had so much fun. Enjoy your home and your hospitality today.

Love,

Michelle

Be ReVITALized
MOTHERHOOD THOUGHT FOR THE DAY: 57

Wound Up

Sometimes I learn best by illustration.

I was recently thinking aobut how easily we can get wound up as wives and mothers, I was reminded of those various wind-up toys—the kind that you have to keep winding up, because they unwind so quickly.

God showed me that I need to be like that. If I get wound up, I need to unwind quickly. I cannot stay all wound up, as that is unhelpful.

Today, let's stay unwound.

Love,

Michelle

It's Kind of a Big Deal

I'm awake. Again. No big deal. Here's how it happened:

- 10:30 pm—went to bed and nursed baby to sleep
- 11:00 pm—my 3-year-old crawled into my bed to crash
- 1:00 am—got up to await older children's return home
- 2:30 am – went back to bed
- 3:00 am—woke up to feed the baby
- 5:00 am—our 6-year-old crawled into bed with us
- 5:30 am—fed the baby again
- 6:30 am—heard our oldest getting ready for work
- 8:00 am—woke up for good
- 8:01 am—thought, "UGH! I'm going to be tired today."
- 8:02 am—but then I remembered...

Someday my house will be quiet. It will also be clean. No little hands will search for me in the night. No little baby will cry for my milk. My kids will all be grown and living in homes of their own. I remembered how as a young mom I'd push three kids in a double stroller. I thought it was hard at the time, but recall the days fondly now. Our days pass so quickly, never to return! Uninterrupted sleep is a luxury, but so is having a house full of children, a home filled with love. Rather than grouse over my lack of sleep, I'll greet the morning with a bright smile and a grateful heart, and do what I can to make this day amazing. And that's kind of a big deal.

Love,

Michelle

Be ReVITALized
MOTHERHOOD THOUGHT FOR THE DAY: 59

Enjoy!

This poem from the book *Great Women of the Bible: Martha*
really spoke to me, and I hope it will bless you, too:

"Lord of pots and pans and things, since I've no time to be
A saint by doing lovely things or watching late with thee
Or dreaming in the twilight or storming heaven's gates.
Make me a saint by getting meals or washing up the plates.
Although I must have Martha's hands, I have Mary's mind...
When I black the boots and shoes, Thy sandals, Lord, I find.
I think of how they trod the earth what time I scrub the floor,
Accept this meditation, Lord, I haven't time for more.
Warm all the kitchen with thy love & light it with thy peace
Forgive me all my worrying and make all grumbling cease.
Thou who didst love to give men food, in room or by the sea
Accept this service that I do—I do it unto thee."

Love,
Michelle

It Doesn't Have to Be Perfect!

Mary certainly did not have the perfect birth plan, with the perfect midwives in attendance, at the perfect, most grand birthing centre around.

God proved to us all that we do not need anything to look a certain way in order for it to be awesome and amazing. So what if circumstances aren't ideal? So what if the house isn't perfect? So what if others think it's crazy?

God is certainly in the details, and He shines in the weakness of them, just as He did in the Bethlehem stable. He showed up quietly and humbly in an animal shelter, yet it was miraculous and spectacular.

Never be tempted to think that you or your circumstances are not measuring up somehow, because your measuring stick is not His.

Love,

Michelle

What Can I Give?

I don't have much to give, or offer,
There are no funds filling the coffer.
My worldly possessions are quite few,
Not of much value in most folks' view.
I only have myself, so weak and sinful,
Falling often, and not the best example.
I'm not world renowned or given to fame,
But I'm still able to proclaim Your Name.
I can offer my womb and the life You may give
To raise in Your Word, and to teach how to live.
I will try to love, to serve, and daily pray
With hope that "Good Servant" You will one day say.
Of Your praises I will frequently sing
To please You with this humble offering.

Love,

Michelle

The Apple of His Eye

Sometimes God's love towards us is compared to a father's love for his children.

That is a fair analogy.

I like to also compare it to a child's love for his mother. A mother is loved, despite her many weaknesses and shortcomings, unconditionally by her child.

A mother is longed for by her child, who adores being in relationship with her and staying constantly at her side.

A mother is truly the apple of her child's eye.

What a great and significant place to be!

Love,

Michelle

Be ReVITALized
MOTHERHOOD THOUGHT FOR THE DAY: 63

A Rare Thing

Rare things are special, aren't they? Here is something that was said to me that is quite rare.

Two of our daughters were performing at an event, and some volunteers were needed. I suggested in a message that some of my adult children could help. One of the organizers replied, and I quote: "I just messaged Kim to see if she still needs some help. Thanks for having so many children."

Did you see that? Incredible! I was thanked for having a large family! That is a very rare and special thing.

Love,

Michelle

Be ReVITALized
MOTHERHOOD THOUGHT FOR THE DAY: 64

What Are We Building?

I would like to produce maternity t-shirts that say: "Pardon my progress. I am building tomorrow's future today."

When we are carrying new life, we are building the future! We are building the nation! We are building the kingdom!

How incredibly amazing is that? Find a pregnant lady to congratulate today.

Love,

Michelle

Be ReVITALized
MOTHERHOOD THOUGHT FOR THE DAY: 65

The Secret Weapon

I like to think of motherhood as being a secret weapon in God's army.

While the world often disregards and disrespects Mother's work, she is quietly building, training, strengthening and sharpening future soldiers.

It makes me think of 1 Corinthians 1:25, because so often His wisdom appears foolish to the world. I smile all the more when I hear someone think a woman could have or should have done more with her life than stayed home for her family. It is all the more gratifying for me to know my work seems foolish to the world!

Fellow mothers, we are secret and powerful weapons—worth more than the world will ever know.

Love,

Michelle

Be ReVITALized
MOTHERHOOD THOUGHT FOR THE DAY: 66

Oh What a Feeling!

One of the very best sensations in the world? Feeling your baby move and kick inside of you.

These are fleeting days that will forever be treasured. What a privilege to carry new life!

Love,

Michelle

Be ReVITALized
MOTHERHOOD THOUGHT FOR THE DAY: 67

Mission Fields

I love to hear missionary stories of life on the field overseas.

However, I also love to hear missionary stories of life on the home front.

We are all missionaries, and we are all on the field! Some of us are paid by an organization to be missionaries, and some of us are missionaries as parents and mentors.

Both are life works worthy of commendation and recognition! One is not higher than the other!

How is the harvest going in your mission field? Planting lots?

Love,

Michelle

Once Upon a Time

In her book, *The Well-Adjusted Child*, Rachel Gathercole shares this thought:

> *"Once upon a time, all children were homeschooled. They were not sent away from home each day to a place just for children, but lived, learned, worked, and played in the real world, alongside adults and other children of all ages."*

This is true, regardless of how you feel about homeschooling today. It is definitely food for thought, and counters the "I can't wait for the children to get back to school" train of thought.

Love,

Michelle

Be ReVITALized
MOTHERHOOD THOUGHT FOR THE DAY: 69

Pride and Joy

I met a sweet lady at the pool yesterday as we shared a table. She was there with her grandchildren, and commented to me how she loved to take them to the pool or some other special place on regular weekly outings. She told me she felt that the grandchildren would all too soon outgrow her in that role, so she was savoring the season.

She was going to be 70 soon, and as we spent the afternoon together watching our children, guess what the topic was? Children and grandchildren and great-grandchildren. I have no idea if or where she ever worked, if or where her husband worked, or what they accomplished financially in their lives.

I do know that she has six children—five daughters and one son—ten grandchildren and one great-grandchild so far. I know the ages and names and even some bits of personality of each of her family members.

This is her pride and joy, and it will be ours as well. Everything else will pale in comparison. Raising our children is of the utmost significance. What a blessing!

Love,

Michelle

Showstopper

I listened to a group of several ladies commiserate about how a "surprise" pregnancy had ended up in twins. The mother was 25 with four little ones now, and this was treated as a most unfortunate circumstance. The grandmother shared how she had to be available to help her daughter at least once a week, as the work was staggering.

"Tsk, tsk" was the overall tone of the conversation, and at this point I just couldn't help but interject. I politely interrupted them and shared how I was now carrying our 12th child, and that each time I conceive, I hope and yearn for twins. I told the grandmother that her daughter was living my dream. I let the group know that I would have 20 or more children if I could. I ended this polite intrusion by stating, "At the end of the day, when I am 80, I won't have a career behind me that perhaps netted me some money or a few possessions. Instead I will have children and grandchildren and generations of family to move forward in this life and the next. I really cannot think of doing anything more valuable with my time than raising children and future generations." It was a showstopper, and the whole room of 20 heard an entirely new perspective.

Love,

Michelle

Be ReVITALized
MOTHERHOOD THOUGHT FOR THE DAY: 71

I Feel Popular!

I'm in my home, in constant demand—
Always called, always touched by some small hand.
My husband needs me, the baby, too,
The teens, the middles, it's quite a crew!

I have people wanting my attention all day,
I can barely have a moment of peace to pray.
The chaos, the work, the constant conversation;
I cannot think of a more gratifying station.

I'm as popular as I can possibly be,
And this life I live is the best for me.
Motherhood and running our home,
Actually makes me feel like I sit on a throne!

To be so needed, so loved, so crucial,
There's nothing else that could be as special.
Popular? Why yes, indeed.
I'm in my home planting good seed.

Love,

Michelle

Be ReVITALized
MOTHERHOOD THOUGHT FOR THE DAY: 72

Sharing Stories, Changing Perspectives

I have a fine story to share with you. My oldest daughter, who is 21, seemed to dread being asked about her family by classmates and coworkers. She was almost apologetic whenever she had to tell people that she's one of 12 siblings.

Recently, we moved to a new house in a new neighbourhood called *The Legends*. I jokingly told the children that one day, we'd BE the Legends. I said as we grow, we'll take over the community—buying houses, having children, and running businesses—we'll BECOME the Legends. Everyone thought this was quite funny. However, I like to give my kids a vision of what the future could be like.

A few days later, my daughter was asked once again about the size of her family. She got the typical reaction of how 12 is too many and it must be such a drag to live with all those siblings. How dreadful for her! But this time, she responded to those comments in a new way: "Actually I see it differently than that," she said. "I see us growing up, buying homes, and establishing families and businesses. Eventually we won't just LIVE in *The Legends*, we'll BE the Legends."

Now, that is much better than her previous responses! I just love how simply sharing stories can change perspectives.

Love,

Michelle

Are You Discouraged?

Sometimes life seems filled with one stress after another, and it feels like there's no end to the grief. Married life may not be blissful and children may become wayward or rebellious. Weary mommas feel worn down. And then we commiserate together. We can go on and on about all we have to contend with.

Can I speak frankly? We need to stop it. Life is full of hardship for all of us. There is no greener grass on any other side. Our self-pity will only serve to make any hardship all the harder. There is good reason that the Word tells us to focus on the positive (Philippians 4:4-8), as the negative wants to eat us alive. But we won't let it!!

We are mothers. Wives. Queens of our Homes. We will not be taken down. We will reign on through it all! We will not succumb to our feelings and most certainly not to our ever-changing circumstances. We'll walk in hope. We'll believe even when we cannot see. We will win. We are not alone. If God is with us, who can be against us (Romans 8:31)?

Victory is ours, dear Mothers. Believe it and repeat it as necessary. We cannot and will not lose, no matter what.

Love,

Michelle

Selfishness Encouraged?

When did selfishness become acceptable?

The other evening I had a conversation with a gentleman who was taken aback by the fact I am expecting our 12th. He told me he had raised three, and had done a lot of coaching and all the other "daddy" stuff, but now, at this time of his life, he felt it was "me time."

As I paused to consider my response, he said that perhaps that seemed selfish, but that he had been a good dad. I said that I could appreciate that people need some time to themselves, but that my focus is more generational. At the end of the day I want generations moving forward more than I want time to myself.

I thought to myself as we parted how we as a culture have lost our vision for our future and turned our focus onto ourselves instead. Is it truly gratifying in the long run?

Love,

Michelle

Be ReVITALized
MOTHERHOOD THOUGHT FOR THE DAY: 75

Rest????

Sweet, weary Momma, in the midst of the messiness of life, I pray you'll find rest.

Rest, you ask?

Yes, rest. *Real* rest for your soul.

We must remember we need not carry more than we are able. Nor do we have to fix more than we can or manage more than we can. We can enter into that wonderful rest of knowing that the One who can manage it all, is indeed managing all of it, perfectly.

We don't need to feel any pressure to be super woman or to see results according to our frail human calculations. We need to enter into His rest, and in that blessed rest, we will accomplish so much more.

We can quit pushing, stressing, and running ourselves ragged. He has us covered, even when we can't see it at the moment. That is faith's blessed rest.

Love,

Michelle

A Baby

There is no better present in the world, and no gift that is more fun to anticipate.

A baby is the greatest gift that life can bring.

Love,

Michelle

Be ReVITALized
MOTHERHOOD THOUGHT FOR THE DAY: 77

Enduring or Enjoying?

I was grocery shopping with the baby the other day when a girl made a comment to me that really got me thinking.

She said that she'd noticed how much I was enjoying my baby and that I was just glowing, and she thought to herself, "that must be her first baby."

I found that strange, as why would I enjoy my first baby more than any other? I enjoy my babies not because of how many there are, or are not, but simply because of the fact that they exist. They are my precious gifts to raise, to love, to teach, and to train.

It really is not about whether that child makes choices later in life that give me joy or sadness, as my job remains the same. I am gifted to be that child's mother, and first, second, tenth, or twelfth baby, I am smitten with love and joy every time, all the time. After all, motherhood is meant to be enjoyed, not simply endured—isn't it?

Love,

Michelle

Be ReVITALized
MOTHERHOOD THOUGHT FOR THE DAY: 78

Let Go and Let God

I hear this so often, but I rarely see it lived out. As I was driving yesterday with a vanload of children, I realized anew that as a parent, I can guide but I cannot control. I was granted great peace as I was reminded that my God IS big enough for all of my children's questions, doubts, challenges, and choices. I do not need to hold on with a death grip, struggling to control their every thought and move. My God can handle them and He is big enough.

I was humbled at how little my faith was in His capabilities. If your children at times scare or shock you with their questions or choices, be encouraged to know that you really and truly can "let go and let God." He is big enough to handle it. He will do an amazing job! Just keep guiding them, and let go and let God be in control, while you rest in peace.

As your children grow up, you will need to more and more entrust them to His most capable care.

Love,

Michelle

As We Talk along the Way

I had a conversation with my 7-year-old daughter today. She stated that she only wanted one child, so there would never be any fighting or yelling.

I replied that one child could be lonely, as that child may end up wishing for brothers and sisters. I also said that since God gives babies, was she going to tell God, "No, don't give me any more babies!"?

She looked astonished and said, "That would be crazy! If God gave me a baby, I would say thank you!"

I sure hope this was one of those teachable moments in her life. I would love for her to be blessed with a husband and babies when she's grown, or at least to be open to the idea of embracing children.

Love,

Michelle

Great Quote

Here's some food for thought:

> *"Where society is rightly ordered, children are regarded, not as an encumbrance, but as an inheritance; and they are received, not with regret, but as a reward."*
>
> - C.S. Spurgeon

Looks like our society has gotten some vitally important things out of order, doesn't it?

Love,

Michelle

Want to Be an Awesome Mom?

Want to be an awesome mom? Then allow yourself the freedom to fail and be imperfect.

I bet you didn't expect me to say that, did you?

Well, by doing so, you show your children not only where to turn when they err, but you also show them that God is the One who can bring healing and strength.

In your weakness, He shines through strong to your children. Perfection has no need of salvation. Too often children have the impression that we parents have it mostly together, and that they are the only ones needing constant correction.

How freeing it is to realize that a facade of perfection is unnecessary for being an awesome parent? We only need to show our children how to walk moment by moment, as a sinner saved by grace. After all, seeing them grow and walk with the Lord is our greatest goal, as we are all sinners in need of grace.

Be free to fail and know that you are more than awesome, and doing an awesome job.

Love,

Michelle

Be ReVITALized
MOTHERHOOD THOUGHT FOR THE DAY: 82

Happiest of Days to You!

A mother's joy is very often wrapped up within the joy and walk of her children. We are thrilled when our children are thrilled. We delight in their delight. When a child recognizes and values the deep love of a mother, a mother's heart is on fire with love and thankfulness.

Two of my favourite quotes about motherhood are as follows:

> *"I remember my mother's prayers and they have always followed me. They have clung to me all my life."*
>
> -Abraham Lincoln

> *"I thought my mom's whole purpose was to be my mom. That's how she made me feel."*
> - Natasha Gregson Wagner

May the Lord bless you tremendously this day, and make His face shine upon you and be gracious unto you, and give you deep and abiding peace. May you take joy in both your own mother and your motherhood.

Love,

Michelle

Be ReVITALized
MOTHERHOOD THOUGHT FOR THE DAY: 83

The Tide Changes

Do you ever get the kind of questions our family hears:

"Are you done yet?"
"Don't you know what causes this?"
"Are you seriously pregnant again?"
"All from the same parents?"
"Haven't you ever heard of birth control?"
"Better you than me!"
"What does your husband do for a living?"

Give it a few years, and the questions and comments begin to take a different tone:

"Wow, you look amazing for that many children!"
"I admire you!"
"You should be on America's Got Talent"
"I wish I could have had more."
"You are amazing!"
"Good for you!"

The tide eventually changes. In the meantime, just ride out the waves!

Love,

Michelle

Be ReVITALized
MOTHERHOOD THOUGHT FOR THE DAY: 84

What's the Worth?

Do you ever feel like your work and contributions as a mother aren't worth very much? Perhaps you believe your female counterparts in the workforce are contributing to society more?

I could say so much about this, but I will with this quote from a report I recently read:

> *"Salary.com surveyed more than 8,000 moms to find out how much time they spend on common tasks, and calculated the pay they would get for managing the same services in the corporate arena. For example, being the CEO of the household comes out to a salary of $171,824 a year or $55.07 an hour."*

Well, now, not too many folks are working for $55 an hour, and although you do not get an actual paycheque as a stay-at-home mom, it is nice to know the financial value of the work you do—not to mention the incredible value of building future generations!

Best wishes to all you wonderful mothers out there for an equally wonderful day!

Love,

Michelle

The Ultimate Career

"The homemaker has the ultimate career.
All other careers exist for one purpose only—
and that is to support the ultimate career. "
- C.S. Lewis.

I especially enjoy that this quote is spoken from a male perspective. Being a homemaker truly is the ultimate career, the ultimate adventure, the ultimate lifestyle, the ultimate experience. Embrace it for all of its wonderfulness!

Even if you are not presently a homemaker full time, it is still your most ultimate career, above any other one. It may rarely offer an actual paycheque, as other careers do, but the earthly joys and the eternal rewards that accompany this vocation are immeasurable!

I just love my ultimate career.

Love,

Michelle

Pro-Life Work?

When Mother Teresa of Calcutta was asked by a young mother about the best way to proceed with pro-life work, she responded emphatically, "Have a big family. That is the best way to end abortion!"

Even if we cannot conceive, we can still raise and/or influence many children for the Lord.

Love,

Michelle

Not Worth Much?

I grew up in a culture where being a "stay at home mum" gave off the impression that the mum must be fairly uneducated and unable to do much else with her life, hence she "just" stayed home.

What a complete and utter falsehood!

Running a home smoothly, training children through all stages of life, figuring out how to feed a growing family with nourishing and wholesome food, and being a godly wife can require more skill and much greater versatility than many high-paying professions.

Stay at home mums need to be experts in far more than one field. It takes endurance, perseverance, diligence, wisdom, passion, research, and so much more. How can anyone believe that a stay at home mum is for the weak-minded?

Stay at home mums are among the very most gifted and competent members of society. And that's the truth.

Love,

Michelle

Dear Fellow Mother...

Dear Fellow Mother,

When you feel worn out, exhausted, taken advantage of, under appreciated and unacknowledged, remember this: The greatest gift of all time came at a very high cost on a wooden cross. We mothers labour not in vain. We are in the trenches together, waging war against all that seeks to defeat us, and trudging forward to great victory.

Of course, there will be some hardships, but we are not failing. We offer the greatest gift that we can—our labour of love to raise godly seed and our commitment to live as an example in our marriages of Christ and His bride.

We are daughters of the King. In every circumstance, being polished by His hand, standing together, arm in arm, and looking up, we'll win.

Love,

Michelle

Fountain of Youth

Whenever someone comments to me that I look too young to have 12 children, I respond that if you have enough children, you end up looking like one—sort of like the saying goes that dogs resemble their owners. It is always good for a laugh.

Science tells us though, that pregnancy hormones are as beneficial to the mother as they are to the baby. The keep a woman looking young and make her complexion glow and her hair thick and glossy.

I suppose the veritable fountain of youth may just be carrying new life. Just one more reason to shout hallelujah!

Love,

Michelle

Be ReVITALized
MOTHERHOOD THOUGHT FOR THE DAY: 90

View of a Young Man

Here my son Bryson shares his perspective on birth control:

People all over the world, even Christians, will not support abortion, but will support birth control. Professional pastors will advise young couples to use the pill. Their reasoning is, "You have to use common sense" or "I can't handle a bunch of children." Hold on there. As Christians we are called to trust the Lord—so why do we trust the Lord with everything except children? Where in the Bible does it say to rely on our own understanding? Or that man's wisdom is sufficient? The answer is nowhere. That's right, nowhere in the Bible will you find a verse that says anything along those lines. The Lord will take care of us, He knows what's best for us, and He will not give us more than we can handle. Let me ask you something, if the Lord gave you ten dollars everyday for the rest of your life, when would you say, "That's enough Lord, I have enough money"? You probably wouldn't. But aren't children more valuable than money? And yet I'll bet you that a lot of people would take ten dollars instead of a child. So I challenge you, Pastors, brothers, and sisters in our Lord, don't use the pill, but trust the Lord. He will take care of you.

Love,

Michelle

Moses Ministers Mightily

Lately, I've felt a little defeated. It seems that regardless how much effort I exert, the work and demands of family life never end. Sometimes it's a struggle to "keep on keeping on." That's how I felt yesterday, but this morning God used Moses' example in Deuteronomy 31 to encourage me. Poor Moses. He spent a great portion of his life teaching the Israelites, then exhorts them in this passage once again. He tells them plainly about the blessings or curses that will befall them, dependent on their conduct. There is nothing wrong with his teaching—it is clear and concise. Yet the Lord warns Moses that the Israelites will not listen. They'll forsake God and reject all that they've been taught.

If anyone had cause to give up in despair, it would be Moses. But he didn't. He kept faithfully pointing the way. Likewise, God continues His never-ending work with a stubborn and rebellious people, all throughout the ages. How, then, can I despair or feel defeated in my daily tasks? I must continue to teach, to train, to plod on, even doing the same things again and again. Perhaps I'll be ignored or the results of my work may not be what I hoped. That's not the point. The point is that, like Moses, I have a job to do. I'm important in God's plan and want to be faithful in the work He's called me to do.

Love,

Michelle

Be ReVITALized
MOTHERHOOD THOUGHT FOR THE DAY: 92

Verse of the Day

I find one of the most challenging aspects of parenting is finding that perfect balance between showing God's mercy and long-suffering, and His justice and chastisement.

He does not treat us as our sins deserve, being so slow to anger and patient beyond measure, and yet He chastens and disciplines us as well-beloved children. So I take comfort in James 1:5: "If any of you lack wisdom, let him ask of God, that giveth to all men liberally, and upbraideth not; and it shall be given him."

Thankfully, we needn't lean on our own limited and faulty understanding, but can walk instead in His strength and wisdom. He trusted us to raise and train these precious ones that He has granted.

May you find encouragement in this truth today, as I have. I am parenting through all the strifes and storms of life, right along with you!

Love,

Michelle

Be ReVITALized
MOTHERHOOD THOUGHT FOR THE DAY: 93

Refocus

The children are bickering; the house is a mess,
My husband is running late, my head feels the stress!
The dishes are piling high; the laundry is, too,
Dinner will not make itself. Ahhh! So much to do!
My children all arrive home, the baby smiles wide,
My toddler snuggles me close, my heart fills with pride!
My sweet teen makes me some tea and then folds the clothes,
I have supper under way—so what were my woes?
I got caught up in demands, lost sight of the joy.
I forgot how blessed I am—'tis the devil's ploy!
We do have each other and a home of our own.
A family full of love, and God on His throne.
I will not be rustled up, having a full plate.
I will choose the better part, knowing my life's great!

Love,

Michelle

Be ReVITALized
MOTHERHOOD THOUGHT FOR THE DAY: 94

Blessed Wombness

I was having a conversation with a young, single woman regarding pregnancy. She felt that men had it so easy, as women have to deal with their monthly cycles, as well as with pregnancy and post-partum issues.

I was able to share that being a woman is the most amazing thing for so many reasons! Only women can share in the creative power of God by bringing forth new life. Only a woman gets to feel new life move and grow within her. Babies know their mother's smell, voice, and heartbeat even before birth, and are easiest to console by being near their mother. Only women get to suckle and nurture their babies at the breast. Only women get to conceive and have the joy of experiencing pregnancy and birth.

She left with much to think about regarding her very blessed and privileged wombness.

Love,

Michelle

Favorite Funny

Tonight at our family meal table, we asked the children what their favourite funny memory was. There were lots of stories to share, and the entire table was involved.

My favourite was when one of our daughters was quite young. She had been recently potty trained, and I noticed she had changed her pants. I asked her if she had wet them, and she said that she hadn't. So I asked her where her other pants were, and she nonchalantly said they were in her room. I asked her to bring them to me.

A little while later, she came out of her room without the pants, claiming that she simply could not find them. She was, however, now sporting a hat. After quite a search, I was also unable to find the other pants. It took me about an hour to catch on, but we eventually discovered that she had folded the soiled pants up in her hat so that we wouldn't know what happened.

Oh did we laugh! Some moments are just forever etched in our minds, and this is the pulse and beauty of family life. I think it is good to recall the best times frequently.

Love,

Michelle

Be ReVITALized
MOTHERHOOD THOUGHT FOR THE DAY: 96

What Lasts?

Wealth? Although it may at times be true for wealth accumulation, I know an even better and stronger way to build for generations than that. We know from the Word that wealth doesn't last, and the Bible also confirms that we need to *"lay up for [ourselves] treasures in heaven, where neither moth nor rust doth corrupt, and where thieves do not break through nor steal."* (Matthew 6:19-21)

To build something that truly lasts, we need to build generations of godly seed, trained in the truth of God's Word. This is worth more than gold or a storehouse of treasure, and will last eternally—for the Holy Spirit moves in souls, not in financial funds.

Love,

Michelle

Be ReVITALized
MOTHERHOOD THOUGHT FOR THE DAY: 97

The Finest Things

Sure, I could have sought out the best paying career and bought impressive homes and cars. Sure, I could have spent years mastering my field and being highly esteemed by my colleagues. Sure, I could have even spent my time working on my body, with hours at the gym so I could sport that admired six pack. I would then be enjoying all those things that society claims to be the "finer things in life."

Those things just aren't good enough for me though. You could call me high maintenance. I want the "FINEST things in life." I don't want a paycheque, a job, or even a gym membership. I would live in a hut and give up all my comforts for the finest things in life: Faith, family, children, a life spent building relationship with a generational focus—this is life at it's finest. Fulfillment for me comes from living the finest. The "fine things" the world chases would only leave me feeling alone and unfulfilled, when my house was full of things, but my heart and table empty. Some pity me thinking I am missing out on those finer things with the demands of a husband and twelve precious babes. Poor souls! What I have I would not sell for ten trillion dollars. I have the finest things life has to offer! I am far richer than they think, but it has nothing to do with money.

Love,

Michelle

97

Time For a Tune Up

Changing a mindset can be a difficult thing to do, but not for the Lord. Allow me to elaborate with a personal example of His creativeness.

Although we were absolutely ecstatic to be pregnant, I found myself "suffering" through the final weeks in some pain and discomfort. I was well beyond the point of rejoicing and onto the point of "are we there yet?" Sleepless nights, heartburn, pain, swelling, and mobility issues were taking a toll on my mood.

Then one morning, I woke up in real actual pain, requiring an immediate visit to the doctor and antibiotics for a serious infection at 38+ weeks.

"Seriously?" I questioned the Lord. "Were things not already tricky enough right now, without this? And I do not know of anyone that detests medicines more than me, especially pregnant."

I was about to be tuned up. You see, after a day of "enhanced" discomfort and illness, I realized that previously, I had absolutely nothing to complain or grumble about. I was in a whole new realm. I realized this and joked that things can always get worse and that we should be careful what we complain about. I quickly went from a state of questioning why, to praising Him for His infinite wisdom. The medication began its work, and I reverted to the typical bulky feelings of the final days of pregnancy with pure joy and thankfulness! I was suddenly thrilled to have only the normal annoyances to contend with, such as heartburn and general discomfort. I felt energized and able to continue, enjoying each day of pregnancy for all of it's worth.

"Seriously," I said repeatedly to my family and friends, "I am so glad I got ill, because it gave me the perspective change I so desperately needed to enjoy these final days/weeks."

I was then feeling fine, in week 39.

If you know of someone (or if it is you yourself) who needs a tune up, be on the lookout for His creativity in molding you and try to enjoy the ride… and be careful what you complain about!

Love,

Michelle

Which Shall It Be?

When I was younger and my family seemed to be growing much too quickly for most of the people around us, I came across the following poem. I loved to read it to those who questioned what we were doing or why we kept having so many babies.

Which Shall It Be?
(by Ethel Lynn Eliot Beers)

Which shall it be? Which shall it be?
I look'd at John; John look'd at me
(Dear, patient John, who loves me yet
As well as though my locks were jet).
And when I found that I must speak,
My voice seem'd strangely low and weak:
"Tell me again what Robert said?"
And then I, listening, bent my head.
"This is his letter:

'I will give
A house and land while you shall live,
If, in return, from out your seven,
One child to me for aye is given.'"
I look'd at John's old garments worn,
I thought of all that John had borne
Of poverty and work and care,

Which I, though willing, could not share;
I thought of seven mouths to feed,
Of seven little children's need,
And then of this.

*   "Come, John," said I,*
"We'll choose among them as they lie
Asleep;" so, walking hand in hand,
Dear John and I survey'd our band.
First to the cradle lightly stepp'd,
Where the new, nameless baby slept,
"Shall it be Baby?" whispered John.
I took his hand and hurried on
To Lily's crib,

*   Her sleeping grasp*
Held her old doll within its clasp.
Her dark curls lay like gold alight,
A glory 'gainst the pillow white.
Softly the father stooped to lay
His rough hand down in loving way,
When dream or whisper made her stir,
And huskily said John, "Not her!"

We stopped beside the trundle bed
And one long ray of lamplight shed
Athwart the boyish faces there,
In sleep so pitiful and fair;
I saw on Jamie's rough, red cheek,
A tear undried. Ere John could speak,
"He's but a baby, too," said I,
And kissed him as we hurried by.

Pale, patient Robbie's angel face
Still in his sleep bore suffering's trace;
"No, for a thousand crowns, not him,"
We whispered, while our eyes were dim.

Poor Dick! bad Dick! our wayward son,
Turbulent, reckless, idle one—
Could he be spared? "Nay, He who gave,
Bids us befriend him to the grave;
Only a mother's heart can be
Patient enough for such as he;
And so," said John, "I would not dare
To send him from her bedside prayer."

Then stole we softly up above
And knelt by Mary, child of love.
"Perhaps for her 'twould better be,"
I said to John. Quite silently,
He lifted up a curl astray
Across her cheek in willful way,
And shook his head, "Nay, love, not thee,"
The while my heart beat audibly.

Only one more, our eldest lad,
*Trusty and truthful, good and glad_*
So like his father. "No, John, no.
I cannot, will not let him go."

And so we wrote in courteous way,
We could not give one child away,
And afterward, toil lighter seemed,
Thinking of that of which we dreamed;
Happy, in truth, that not one face
We missed from its accustomed place;
Thankful to work for all the seven,
Trusting the rest to One in heaven!

I loved this poem when I first read it and still do. I hope that
you enjoyed it, too.

Love,

Michelle

Pro-Choice?

Sure I'm "pro-choice," what can I say?
I get to make my own choices every day.
I choose to live my life as a believer you see,
And that means the Bible reveals how I should be.
It means I respect life at every stage of the game.
From conception to the grave, it's all the same.
The Creator makes each one so individual,
And each life truly is such a miracle!
Why would I interfere with His creative power?
The very thought of trying to makes me want to cower!
HE knows best, I know this full well,
So resting in His will makes me feel just swell.
And being "pro-choice," I get to choose each day
How to live my life in a way that'll really pay.
So each day I choose to submit to my role
As a wife and a mother, and I feel totally whole.
It is so fulfilling, and challenging, too,
There is never a dull moment in our family "zoo."
Sometimes I even choose to bite my tongue
And that keeps my marriage much more fun.
I sometimes choose to serve selflessly
And those are the days that I really feel free.
I can also choose to praise instead of criticize
Following that advice is a good word to the wise.

I love all of the choices I get to make.
Nothing about them makes me feel fake.
I have chosen the good path, of this I am sure;
For there is no other workable cure.
To live this life full of sin and pain
I need God's grace to remove my stain.

Love,

Michelle

About the Author

Michelle Kauenhofen is a Bible-believing wife to one and a momma to many. She adores her family, with her amazing husband, six sons, and six daughters. She loves—and I do mean *loves*—life in general, and tries not to take moments for granted. She makes it her habit to look for the best in all situations and (especially) in all people. She makes her home in Canada, although she longs for sand, sun, and sea (and deep down, she despises snow and doesn't even care that much for hockey—*gasp!*).

The riveting question at the time of this book printing was, "If Michelle does not get pregnant again... then what?" The answer birthed *The ReVITALizing Ministry* and *THE ReVITALizing WOMEN CONFERENCES*. Her high energy must be put to use somewhere, and interacting with folks and speaking life into relationships is what she loves to do.

You'll find Michelle online at www.revitalizingwomen.com.

Also from Prescott Publishing

25 Ways to Communicate Respect to Your Husband:
A Handbook for Wives
by Jennifer Flanders

100 Days of Blessing:
Devotions for Wives and Mothers (Volumes 1 and 2)
by Nancy Campbell

Cheer Up:
Motivating Messages for Each Day of the Year
by Michelle Kauenhofen and Nancy Campbell

Glad Tidings:
The First 25 Years of Flanders Family Christmas Letters
by Jennifer Flanders

How to Encourage Your Children:
Tools to Help You Raise Mighty Warriors of God
by Nancy Campbell

How to Encourage Your Husband:
Ideas to Revitalize Your Marriage
by Nancy Campbell

Love Your Husband/ Love Yourself:
Embracing God's Purpose for Passion in Marriage
by Jennifer Flanders

The Prodigy Project: A Novel
by Doug Flanders, MD

Want to ReVITALize Your Marriage?

Check out these books

Love Your Husband/ Love Yourself: Embracing God's Purpose for Passion in Marriage (Jennifer Flanders)

If you've ever caught yourself making excuses to avoid physical intimacy with your spouse or viewing sex as a duty rather than a privilege, this book will forever change your perspective. More a "why to" book than a "how to" book, *Love Your Husband* will open your eyes to all the amazing physical, mental, and psychological benefits available to couples who fully embrace God's purpose for passion in marriage.

25 Ways to Communicate Respect to Your Husband: A Handbook for Wives (Jennifer Flanders)

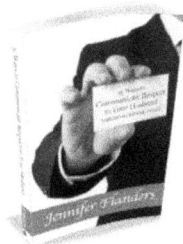

We get out of marriage what we pour into it:

Would you like for your husband to be more attentive? Do you long for him to notice and admire you? Do you wish he'd recognize and appreciate all you do? Do you want him to be respectful of your wishes and opinions? Would you like for him to spend more time with you? Then treat him as you want to be treated!

Winner of CSPA's Book of the Year Award!

How to Encourage Your Husband: Ideas to Revitalize Your Marriage (Nancy Campbell)

Looking for fresh ideas for strengthening you marriage and building up your man? Then this is the book for you. It contains a treasure trove of easily-implemented tips, collected and compiled by Nancy Campbell, who has devoted the past 35+ years to encouraging wives and mothers around the world, in true Titus 2 fashion.

www.ingramcontent.com/pod-product-compliance
Lightning Source LLC
Chambersburg PA
CBHW060946040426
42445CB00011B/1022